Advance Praise for
Intact

Claudia Masin is one of the most original voices surging forth from contemporary Argentine poetry. And now English-language readers have the moment to experience the electric lurch once a body is brought back from death, all thanks to the lucidity, accuracy, and unflinching probity from one of our most talented contemporary translators and poets, Robin Myers. *Intact* opens with poems kicking up the dust of some other existence, where we—the readers, Myers, Masin—are no longer locked in our bodies, or aren't even members of our species, but somewhere else, a space of yearning. We enter the language in Myers' spellbinding English, as one enters pain that proves to be a beautiful landscape. The overarching architecture that builds the collection's narrative thrust is a suite of films. The films provide clips, texts, and tableaux by such diverse directors as Abel Ferrara, Ingmar Bergman, and even *Magnolia* by Paul Thomas Anderson. (Poetry lovers and cinephiles, Masin's book beckons you!) And just as images flicker in the dark against the silver screen, the poetry in this book, stirring in the estuary between Spanish and English, in that magical space that can never be precisely discerned, in what can never be touched, yet unearths memories from earliest childhood, and before. Call it music. Call it poetry.

—**Anthony Seidman**, translator of
CONTRA NATURA by Rodolfo Hinostroza

Masin inhabits language with the ease of a stream, but she follows the frenetic rhythm of a stormy sea. It's no exaggeration to say that each of these poems is a universe unto itself, a space that demands new eyes.

Stop there, don't move, and let her words look back at you. Can you see how they pulse, how they urge us to behold the blade of language, of the imagination?

—**Isabel Zapata**, author of *IN VITRO*

INTACT

CLAUDIA MASIN

TRANSLATED BY
ROBIN MYERS

Intact

FLOWERSONG
PRESS

poems by
Claudia Masin

translated by
Robin Myers

FLOWERSONG
PRESS

For Carolina Cadamuro

I wanted to stay as I was
still as the world is never still,
not in midsummer but the moment before
the first flower forms, the moment
nothing is as yet past—

—Louise Glück

For what there is to tell about is what was not seen...*and this is all your chore. What is not seen torments the eye as though eye were only a ball of glass in a socket, until the brain can build an image of what is unseen and give vision to the eye.*

—William Goyen

Acknowledgements

"Tomboy" was among the winners of the 2019 Poems in Translation Contest held by *Words Without Borders* and the Academy of American Poets. It was published in *WWB* and featured in the AAP's Poem-A-Day series.

"Magnolia" appeared in *The Common*.

"The Silent Touch," "Hideaways," "4:44," "Perfect Sense," "Persona," "Once," "Summertime," and "Nazareno Cruz and the Wolf" were published in *Caesura*.

table
of contents

Intact

Tomboy

I don't understand how we walk around the world
as if there were a single way for each of us, a kind
of life stamped into us like a childhood injection,
a cure painstakingly released into the blood with every passing year
like a poison transmuted into antidote
against any possible disobedience that might
awaken in the body. But the body isn't mere
submissive matter, a mouth that cleanly swallows
whatever it's fed. It's a lattice
of little filaments, as I imagine
threads of starlight must be. What can never
be touched: that's the body. What lives outside
the law when the law is muscled and violent,
a boulder plunging off a precipice
and crushing everything in its path. How do they manage
to wander around so happily and comfortably in their bodies, how
do they feel so sure, so confident in being what they are: this blood,
these organs, this sex, this species? Haven't they ever longed
to be a lizard scorching in the sun
every day, or an old man, or a vine
clutching a trunk in search of somewhere
to hold on, or a boy sprinting till his heart
bursts from his chest with sheer brute energy,
with sheer desire? We're forced
to be whatever we resemble. Haven't
you ever wished you knew what it would feel like to have claws

or roots or fins instead of hands, what it would mean
if you could only live in silence
or by murmuring or crying out
in pain or fear or pleasure? Or if there weren't any words
at all and so the soul of every living thing were measured
by the intensity it manifests
once it's set free?

The Silent Touch

It's not the soul. It's not an immaterial being, a gust
that fills the body: the mystery is the body in itself,
its complex myriad of veins,
the blood that rushes forth to feed the organs,
hidden like prehistoric animals in caverns so secluded
that only illnesses can find them.
Contact with others is what heals,
what sickens, the sun
encircled by the lonely planet
of ourselves, caught in the orbit
of the light or shadow as they draw
their heat toward us or away, as if we were
the dust kicked up by some other existence, the wake
churned at the source, the indissoluble bond we were supposed to renounce
but which awoke again each time we loved
another body. You hoped I'd write the words
that can do what music does:
step through the silence without harming it, be
part of it, and of the things that can't be said,
the things we can't even approach without
them darting away from us. I told you there's nothing
like music but touch
and being touched, the particles
that meet and fuse and sometimes scrape against each other and
cause pain, and pull away, and sometimes one explodes
inside the other, because there's neither surface

nor interior: the inside is the same as out. Inside,
the love we share or cruelty we inflict plunge down into a well
and can't climb out again. We were gifted this fall
so that we would collide, one dashed against another,
so that we'd have
to mark each other.
And once we've got our mark, we'll never be alone; we couldn't
be unbroken even if we wanted to.

Estuaries

Once, humans hunted the animals of the estuaries
in the siesta's radiant calm.
The steel of the sun and the weapons sank
into still water. Now
people let them live: a kind concession, a gift
the mighty grant their servants. The alligators
can emerge, like us,
and sprawl for hours in the heat, tired
old lizards placidly abiding
the birds who settle on their hides to rest before
they fly away. The piranhas,
like all good furtive, implacable creatures,
throng close around the shoals and patiently await
their prey. The lives of foxes and roe deer
are spared; it's now forbidden
to delight in their terror, their desperate,
doomed attempt to blend into the brush. You and I
were wild once, but we weren't so lucky:
only when no one else was watching
could we roam free without an ambush, without some sudden
teeth wrenching the joy
from our flesh. But we weren't scared.
We snatched the sustenance we'd been refused,
and we ran riot,
fleeing the time that gained on us,
the time when we'd be sundered by the law

7

declaring that the only possible passions between two boys—
or men—
are cruelty, rage, and violence. So how did we escape,
how did the hunter overlook us,
how did a love survive inside our chests,
deadeye as the stone that could
have felled us with a single throw?
I don't know how we stay
alive, those of us
who were never fated to exist. Maybe it's
the strength sparked when we join together,
the boundless force that means we cease to be
a pair of solitary beasts, each one the only sample of its kind, born ready
for extinction.

Origins

In the limbo between life and death,
say certain holy books, comes liberation:
at last, you understand. Is understanding freedom, then?
Understanding as stones do, stripped of souls,
light in their roughness, delivered
into the passion that the elements
unleash upon them: the hail's assault,
the wind's sensual brush, the savagery
of the sun, which sears and turns them
into smoldering embers
until the rain blows in and licks them clean
as the lioness bathes her cubs
when they're born. At last, you understand (so say the books)
that death doesn't exist, or at least
death as point
of no return. You always return.
Would I recognize you if you came back
as the little girl selling flowers
on the streets of Mumbai, or as the agile, grim-faced buck
the hunter tracks at dawn, or the monk who tends
his garden in the mountains where nobody
can see it, or the guerrilla fighter with a shield
of explosives strapped to himself in a busy market, or the tree
contorting at the cliff's edge, lengthening its limbs
in search of a little sun, deformed by the strain, by the lust
for staying alive? I just don't know

if I'd be able to recognize you
without the face, the matter
so familiar to my eyes and hands. But I do know
that as soon as I found you,
the fragile ice would crack
beneath my feet again, and the fierce blow
of frozen water would jolt me awake, as the body awakes
once it's dead and then absorbs
the electric lurch that shocks it back to life.

Lost Girls

I follow you. I'm the shadow of a body that's gone
when I arrive: your body, which transformed so instantly into another
that only I knew it was you. You were
the stranger, her, him, left eternally outside,
the one who couldn't come back in, the one without
credentials. We tore through the enclosure like
the hunted beasts we were, so ardent was our need to get away
that we effortlessly transposed the limits of the species,
the rules that say you'll never be more than a her, than a him,
a man, a woman, a compliant body
that reluctantly accepts a certain way
of feeling pleasure, the immovable nature
of its suffering. That night, though, you were a medium
who waved off evil spirits with your fingers fixed in one
conclusive gesture. The flower that fertilized itself
and reproduced its rarity, its need to grow
beyond the obstacles, to exploit the light
outside. You were the vegetable, the slave
to what unswervingly awaits submission
and silence and then breaks away and grows in the air
out of sheer imperative desire, your roots
unearthed. You can't survive—
as you'd always been told—without
someone else's water, the nourishment
no rebel will receive. It doesn't
matter; your whole body howled that it didn't matter, that life

and death look much alike if you don't evade the destiny
you were prescribed before your birth,
if you don't cross over to the other side and return
transformed forever
or simply don't come back. I'd love you
in any form you chose: the timid girl
who doesn't raise her voice because it bothers
those who are allowed to speak; the strong-willed boy
the world expects compactness of,
assumes he'll act with violence
and a sense of conquest, as masters do.
But what I came to love you for was that
you chose to stay right where you were, refusing
to take orders or to give them, to be the lord
or servant. And I, who lack the nerve, the courage,
who watch you swallow down the sap that makes you strong,
and watch you spit the poison suckled with your mother's milk,
I'm yours: your woman, your man,
whatever I must be to break the spell,
so we can swim downstream,
against the eddies, without the fear of being swallowed down
into the abyss where the known world will disappear,
the pit, the mouth that hungers endlessly
to devour the defiant in a single gulp.

Hideaways

The only thing I knew
was how to hide out in a world
that saw me merely as an exotic animal,
the last remaining specimen of a rare
and dangerous species. But what to do when someone
looks at you with the softness that replaces
repulsion or fear,
when the touch of someone else's gaze
is an embrace you can't
shake off, and you don't want to pounce
or flee, just linger in its halo like a flame
that checks its power so you won't be burned. What should I do,
who only know to hurt as I was hurt. What should I do with the rage,
with the hatred that impales my chest
like an loosed
arrow. What should I do but close my eyes
and let that gaze, gentle and persistent as a stream,
close my wounds, seep into every battered fiber,
and heal them smooth again, although I know—I know—that nothing
ever becomes what it once was, intact,
nothing can be restored to the moment of
its own fracture. Forgive me, then,
for not knowing how to heal under the touch of your eyes and hands,
forgive me for the pain I will inflict
on you, and for illness and death,

for everything I can't hold back, for what we know to be
an impossible promise,
the one I'll make you even so.

Perfect Sense

We enter pain like someone entering
a beautiful landscape:
something we weren't expecting
suddenly takes our breath away and makes us stop
to look. But not even the sharpest gaze
can understand what's simply there,
what doesn't include us
and expects nothing from us, doesn't want
our awe, our presence. It stays
when we go, remains intact even though
it's changed us forever. You asked me
to detach you from your pain
as a shaman drives evil from
the poisoned body
and cleanse what's been corroded, the toxin's
remnants, the mark life left
when it dissolved into the bloodstream on
the first day, malignant and inexorable as a snakebite
in sleeping flesh. But all I could do, all
I can still do is give you an antidote
that doesn't last and never cures: the press
of skin on skin, the poor
and potent human act of touch.
All will vanish. There won't be any signs to show
that we once met,

we'll leave no proof of either the dread
or the love that brought us close, of those two ties
that were like water in water once:
indistinguishable. There won't be any
eyes to conjure up the colors. We won't know how
to summon back the sound of branches
shifting in the wind, And not a single trace
of cold-scent will persist in us, dead leaves
varnished with frost, and we won't be able to recover
the pleasure of the berries splitting
in our mouths. But even when there's nothing left,
some memory in our touch will bring
it back to us again, as if we'd never lost it:
the moment when another life stepped into ours,
certain and supple as an arrow flung
in flight, and made us understand that we
are matter that will meet an end, and sometimes,
before ending, will be granted the grace
of being hurt in such a way that makes it mortal,
which means it's saved.

Manchester by the Sea

I knew peace once, the sun's
warm gong against the pavement
on a drowsy summer afternoon, bare
feet on pitch, our shouts and laughter hushed
to let our sleeping parents lie. I knew
peace once, although I never had it; it always left me before I could
keep it. And now it's gone. Don't ask me how
the things we never owned
are taken away from us. I only know—I know for sure—that life
clenches my neck like tree rings and I can't
break free of it. I can't
always follow what people say.
Maybe it's the struggle that keeps me quiet
and discreet instead of howling
like a wolf, or maybe it's this jostling exhaustion, layer
upon layer of fatigue. Who could possibly hear another voice
while focused on the almost imperceptible sound
of a new crack,
when the mind is the surface
of a frozen lake that slowly starts
to fissure. Better just surrender to
defeat: that's what I'd like, to split the ice
with one cruel step. If I were a wall, I'd
have fallen in by now, would have succumbed
to gravity. But I
am made of living matter, which is

persistent. I lost
everything I had, and also what I didn't: incredibly,
I still feel love for all this stubborn physicality,
the very faith
with which the oldest, weakest animal
wakes from hibernation and draws a breath
of hot dry air into its lungs, reviving it once more,
as if breathing were still important, even now, when the body
is a hollow, nothing more, a hole through which the world
still comes and goes, leaving no trace.

4:44

Sometimes life, unmediated
by death, just ends. Sure, it starts over again,
but it's not the same: it's like you've cleaved
an axe into tree bark. That's
where all of its fragilities
will gather from now on. A single blow
in that soft place will be enough to fell it. I'd keep watch
day and night so that force wouldn't catch you
by surprise and do you harm. You'd tell me, *I'm not a tree,*
I don't have roots, that means I can survive
any disaster: it's firm and solid bodies
that risk being broken.
I'm more like
a vine that grows in midair. And yet I know, we know,
that perfect storms exist, and those
spare no one. It doesn't matter: that's your faith,
and the faith of those who don't realize they believe
is the strongest kind of all, the only one
that can work miracles. What else would you call the fact
that an unloved body
keeps breathing, if everything we have depends on others,
on their capacity to hold us up, to give us breath?
What else, if not the most ferocious will to live,
would keep a person on their feet
who'd been offered only indifference from the start,
or sheer violence, uncontrollable and deadly? It's the world's

last morning before it shatters, and even now
we're all caught up in little things—that our house,
for example, seems like a house. No matter what you say,
hope keeps laboring on the body, even
when the body gave up long ago and stopped
its wanting. There is an impulse greater
than itself, than you and I, than everything
that will be lost. It's kindled by a fire
that has no origin, no flinting spark, no future, desperate
to incarnate any matter that will let it
keep on burning. An inextinguishable
ember that becomes a lesion
on the body. The grace and passion that belonged to us
will smolder in that wound
after the body is snuffed out: the will-
o'-the-wisp.

It's Only the End of the World

You went as far away as possible to scare off fear,
as if fear had a source, could spring
from some specific place on earth, a geyser, say, and all it took
to keep from getting scalded was to leave its realm forever. But the burn
doesn't want you to be healed; it stings
unendingly. You thought it would be better not have a home,
to be a street dog, fending for itself; to recognize
the smell of food and blood, of sex
and death. You learned your instincts young:
you learned to find a place to lay your head,
alone, free of the herd that saw
the gleam of weakness in your eyes and pushed you
with its wild, collective force into the swamp
of time-before-birth,
so that you'd never think you could belong
to the family of the living. But you came back
and held your mother's body, and your sister's, and that embrace
aspired to be the stalk that would affix you there,
would root you to the ground. And yet no ground
received you. The hand of someone who loves you but doesn't
understand you, the hand
of someone who wants to drive you far
away because your life offends the bedrock of their own—
that hand rested on your chest. And your heart,
a bird-heart apprehended by a stone tossed in the air,
beat hard against the edges of your body

until calm came, the quiet
rhythm of the breath that starts to cease,
to unburden itself, to writhe
against the tumult of the sky and hostile winds
and surrender, finally, to the forces
it had resisted from the start—
and not because it thought it could defeat them,
but just because that was the task, that's what it was there for: it never
had a choice.

Persona

If you refuse to speak, to move, if you decide,
one day, to freeze in place, you bring the universe
to a halt. Everything seems to carry on like always, but a crack
begins to open, and what the world works day and night
to banish filters through: what every body brought here
when it came, what hasn't been restricted to a set
of safe and simple movements that don't break
or threaten the reigning order. What was present before
it disappears forever: the magnificent,
inconceivable force that smashes us against the others and shatters us
and gathers up the splinters and jumbles
them together until there's no way to know where any body starts
and ends. And then a magnet comes, an engine of attraction just as potent as
the one that bears us toward the center of the earth,
and swallows any inkling of rebellion: if you refuse
to be a single he, a single her, isolated and protected from the rest
by a thicker bark than what protects an ancient tree, then you
will lose it all, even the paltry comfort
of words in trying to weather
the scale of the loss. I chose to leave, and I
no longer have a place to live, nor the materials nor the willpower
to rebuild. The wall came down at last;
there's nothing left behind it. You told me we were two
despondent children, full of good intentions
but ruled by powers
that we can't entirely control. And children don't

yet know from pacts; all they can do
is wander barefoot through the snake-infested woods,
ignoring any orders or advice that might relieve them
of a life without hazard, without the ache of someone
else's pain. They're foreign to
the fear-marred apathy that is
the strongest antidote. So may this law, the law of children, be
our own. The law that makes
us smart and shiver in
the storm, the drawn-out suffering
of every injured animal we meet along the way.
Let it be their law that flays and leaves us lacking
words to shelter in. Let us become the creatures we once were, mute
in the face of horror; let us reject,
in sheer brute rage, the forces
that break us into shadows
among other shadows, sundered particles
of radiant light that linger patiently
as they await their smothering, not even lighting up
the tiny, trifling point on earth where they had once,
just for a moment, lived.

The Return

The world is ending all the time. It ended when
I entered the shade of your tree, impossibly vast—and I,
no less than I, sick shrub, branches corroded
by insects and humidity. The sun ended for me,
for everything that seemed to grow in my fragile shadow.
The ground ravaged by pesticides, a scattering of shoots,
acrid in the mouths of nomadic animals,
now lost, who thought they'd tracked the water's course, the river's veins,
only to sink up to their necks
in dense, disloyal clay they'd never emerge from.
I'd never emerge from your shadow, even if I plunged
an axe into your side, even if the axe-blow
were as ruthless as a lightning bolt,
to fell you with a single thud,
to flee your sight toward warmth
before you snared me in your thorns, before
I could leave you behind and strike out on the desolate path, my path,
where I would never hear you, where your calls would never reach me,
bearing me like a magnet toward your life. Each day
you took away my hunger and my bread, the body's will
to health, to live upright. You spoke
the words that would become the food
that never fills, the obverse zeal, the fire of things
that eat themselves. The words that seared like wounds
in a salt rain, the end of the world, the kingdom of horror
and injustice—the only one you saw. The country of the child

so tormented that he couldn't be saved, and even in death
keeps reciting the law imposed on him, the law of hate
that says: all things of beauty
will be inexorably terrible, their skeletons
stripped bare and so eroded that no hope or joy
could ever be tempted. I hold you now, I hold you then,
when you too came into the shade where nothing
and no one makes it out alive. I hold you
so brutally that it's as if I want to hurt you
and yet I'm saving you, saving myself
from horror, I'm telling you
I won't die of the evil that killed you, I'm going
to bring you back to life, even if I have to strike
your chest with my fists
until you breathe again, until you come back with nothing
left to say to me, no hidden dagger, until you become
what you never were or will ever be, the father who resists
the wild urge to swallow down his children and then lets them go
before they grow into your cruelty and your pain
and turn, like you,
into the wounded young that no one,
out of empathy or care,
will ever help to die.

Revenge

for Vega Cerezo

Some people rupture and others repair,
you told me. Sometimes it's just that simple. In the middle
are all the subtleties, and one
is troubling: if all you know is pain,
even you, even once, even by accident, will mend another. And vice-versa.
You told me about a doctor, in a remote part
of Africa, nicknamed the woman-fixer: he works
to patch up women who've been raped. With a strange
and feminine patience, he reconstructs the tissue,
fastens, sews their shattered bodies.
Most of the women are brought to him several times
throughout their lives. Some return
with their daughters. As spoils of war, it's a warrior's privilege
to mutilate them,
the victor's proof of power
over the vanquished. How can we halt the wheel
that hurtles pain toward pain, the harm
that stuns us in the first sting of injustice, the one that makes us wish
maiming and death upon the maimers and the killers? How can
we come to be the ones who cure the plague-
corrupted flesh, our own
and not? How can we dodge the blow
of hate that rises up abruptly like a wind
and makes us into what

we fought against? I don't have the answer. Some questions
burst against the chest: they leave a crater,
a vast, barren expanse where tiny tendrils
might be seen to burgeon after many days
or maybe nothing ever grows at all, except the shoot
of an infinite violence, unsated
by its object, fanning out till it wounds
the others hurt
by similar brutality. We'll have to start all over,
to learn to touch people and things again
as childhood taught us. But instead of the gesture
of appropriation, of growing greed,
might there be a way, a way that doesn't yet exist,
to touch without leaving a wound that will take an age,
a life, to heal—though restitution isn't even
guaranteed? It's all I ask: for us
to cause no further pain than what's already here.
Above all, do no harm, as the first doctors of our tribe
once said.

Against the Wall

Too much that can neither be written nor kept silent!
—Tomas Transtörmer, tr. Robin Fulton

Catastrophes spark everyone's compassion.
An avalanche, a quake, a bombing,
what happens to people's lives when the earth trembles,
the loss of some material reference point enabling
a sequence to continue: night follows day,
the seasons shift, you're sheltered from the elements. But what if
the cataclysm leaves no mark, if it detonates
inside the body when you lack
the words to absorb it into the plot of things?
What if it happens only once, right at the source, and stays there:
alone and monstrous and devastating in its consequences,
echoing forever? You told me once: *I want to bring you back
to where you were before I hurt you.*
And what if where I was didn't exist, love, except
as a time I can only assume was real, a time
I can't remember, so brief I couldn't
keep it? Even then? Even then, would you still want
to struggle to rebuild it, as if you were a member
of a rescue squad arriving at a ravaged town
to clear debris and carry off the dead and close their eyes
so no one else would stop and see
the sordid blemish of surprise and suffering? Would you
still see those bodies and those stones

as evidence of what had been—a tranquil life, the sturdy facts
that people believe in: the prompt and staunch arrival
of heat, cold, work, births, celebrations? Would you still stay
and rebuild houses brick by brick? Would you be just another laborer
among the multitude, spirits unflagging, because despair is absent
from your job description, because they summoned you to fix what's broken
and your only mission is to fight collapse, although you know
collapsing never ends, that everything
we build is razed
by an opposing force that grows
and grows just as we think we've won? If you'd still try it
even so, then I want you to understand it will be like
the choice of somebody who slams her car into a wall and trusts
she will survive: it's the same senseless courage,
the same devotion to impossibilities, the kind—maybe because
they were so forcefully desired—that sometimes even come to pass.

Moonlight

and when we speak we are afraid
our words will not be heard
nor welcomed
but when we are silent
we are still afraid

So it is better to speak
remembering
we were never meant to survive.

—Audre Lorde

Some of us aren't even members of our species
beyond the error, the anomaly confirming the precision
and the balance of things. Like the defective,
sickly pups their mothers pick up by the scruff and set aside,
no strength or courage is expected of us.
There's usually no need to kill us:
the body drained
of others' love and lust is quick to fade. A stain in the sky
that few can spot before it vanishes
thousands of light years away, never touching down to land,
entirely unmissed. But sometimes,
against all odds, a frenzied root grows wild,
suspended in midair until it finds something to clutch,
pulled along by a savage sort of yearning, the thrust of life
persisting even when it knows the feral strain will risk

its rupture. *Rest your head*
in my hands, you told me. *I promise not*
to let you go. And I, who only knew
I ought to dart away from love
like a rock aimed at my chest, a skillful blow
in the weakest place, I let myself
be held regardless and was cured
of others' maladies, of what they'd done with me
to save themselves. I didn't need anyone else to touch me. A body
braced by another body becomes a home.

Once

You knew—how did you know?—that I was broken, shattered
like a struck bone, shards
slashing at everything,
fragmenting what was whole:
a detonation in the center of the earth
eternally warping the perfect cadence of
what will only reach us as an echo now, reverberations,
a distant call that would suffice—if we
could hear it—to heal the ailing
flesh, recover all of what would otherwise
be irretrievable. Maybe that's
the music we all carry with us, and not the constant,
anguished noise the words make when they want
to name a thing they weren't made for. Ear to my chest,
you heard the remnants of the tempo,
cruelly interrupted, that still sounds,
and told me what it sounded like. And in your voice the song
was beautiful: so strong it made me ancient,
a frail and weary tree lashed by a raging gale.
Beauty is violent. Once it slips into your body,
it won't leave you in peace, however hard you try to tear it out,
or look away, stop touching it, absorbing it like a vicious infection
in every cell. You can't be cured of what's too beautiful
because life clings to it, and life's the fiercest,
most stubborn habit of them all. It throws itself at beauty,
which presents a promise of a thing

we've known just once, just briefly. It offers a homecoming,
a return. It vows a fire that won't consume
the bedrock of the house, a house
that won't close up around us
like a set of claws, a hungry mouth,
a body resting from its ruthlessness. It promises a time
when ruthlessness won't be the only way to touch
each other, leave our mark. And who
would turn away from such a pledge.

Sister

I didn't choose you. You don't get to choose an illness
or a mother or a country or a voice
or the intensity of your hatred or
your love. Your sibling is
the one who spells you out: the body
is one word beside the other. If no one can
decipher them, they slump
and die. It's not that they make sense, or form
a lucid phrase—I mean the kind of words
that look more like the sketch of ancient tree roots
on scorched ground. They're like
a map that foxes print in dirt,
prowling through thickets for their prey.
They're like the light-glint of a newborn's eyes
on everything, the gentle brush
of an unfocused, open gaze. They're like
the painful shudder through the muscles of the slave
who bows his head, preparing to receive
his master's violence. You're my sister
because you knew the words that held my body up
weren't the same words that could demolish it. Like the old house
we are, we overflow even in childhood, crammed
with things that weigh us down, objects we wish
we could abandon. But we can't flee
alone when disobedience is punished
(what else?) with loneliness: like horses

who've wandered too far from the stables, sunk to our knees
in quicksand, with no one on their way to lace
their arms around our necks, and pat our flanks, and save us
from the torture of it all. You're my sister
because you came with me as far as anyone
could come: until the end. That liberation,
that other kind of wilderness we do enter alone.

Magnolia

I love the brazen flowers of summer, the kind
we think are either beautiful or simply strange; we're never sure. Too
showy, too eccentric, an explosion, a stain
unfolding, white or red on green, the humdrum green
suddenly burning. If only we were like that too, and not
the shy and fearful people that we are, expanding in our fear
as if fear were the sap, the blood, the food, the root
that tethered us to earth
and somehow both kept us alive and killed us slowly,
since death by fear is never quick:
years, years of fissuring and breaking off
until we're just a naked stalk,
defenseless. If we were like those flowers, I said to you,
the day we first felt pain would be another
ordinary day, and not the nucleus, the source
of everything that followed, the sacred,
necessary fact, the bedrock of the house
we'll build to lock ourselves away and keep
from being damaged once again. If we were more like them, a different
day entirely would be our home. The day
when something happened that defied the laws of logic,
a thing that never should have happened, cannot
happen, happens only in the movies
or in dreams. I crave
the violence of what shows up unannounced, the stone that cracks
the mirror of the wake, the windowpanes, the lightning bolt that could unleash

itself on any object in the world and picks your skull. I long
for an encounter that will cause a new, intolerable pain, uncoupling us
from prior hurt as from a chrysalis, a swath of gauze
wrenched off. I long for your forgiveness, to be
forgiven for the things we never know, for everything
we don't know how to give each other—and I long for us to be able
to recover, later, in the sun, like injured horses,
trampled flowers, expecting nothing but
warm light on withered
petals, on cracked hide. I hope the coming day
will not be beautiful or even happy; please let it be
extraordinary.

Summertime

I look at you: you're sad as if this day
were already the memory of itself, years
from now, when there's no concrete evidence to prove
that it existed. Yet you're alive,
your smile as bright beside me as when you
were young and roamed the town
bared to the elements, the lashing of the lightning
and the rain, daring and joyful at the blade
of summer storms, under the season's wild,
defiant beauty, unyielding even
to the risk of hurt, the chance
that something stronger than your life could drag you out the door
and leave you there. What if the windstorm
could uproot it now, as it did then? What if you lost
your peace and bliss again
to the brute force of an unrepeatable day, a wedge
continuously stuck between your body
and what your body wants? *If someone asked me now,*
you said, *if I'd be willing to endure the trials again*
to reach the day I met you,
I'd say yes. It wasn't raining yet, it wouldn't rain
till it was far too late to think of shelter,
as if you were, we were, what childhood cleaved
in every cell: a kind of wisdom we can't grasp
but which, sometimes, grasps us, and leads us right
to where we need to be, although we can't escape

or defend ourselves, or remember why
we feared so many things so much
or when we'd finally been freed
from fear, from that spectacularly useless flame
that burns unburning.

Melancholia

I'm not the one who wound up hovering in space, unreachable
from earth. It's all of us: no one but animals
and children can be spared, locked in the joy of living,
released only by growing up
or dying. As for the rest of us, what do we know
what winter really smells like, if we can't remember
the slash of cold across the face, the opening
to countless tiny shards of frost, if we've forgotten
the single most important thing: the sensation
of the sun that forced the body's
drawn-out freeze to melt, and what it meant
to stretch out like a jaguar stirring from a nap,
then sprinting off, crazed by the thrill
of waking up at last? If it's not joy,
then may disaster be the force that pulls us from the cave,
and shudders us, and saves us in the end:
the worst thing that could happen isn't death,
isn't the end of the known world. It's living in a limbo
where night and day are indistinguishable, where we can only hope
that life will pass without laying its hands on us, that the others
won't hurt us, that no one will touch us
in such a way that makes us later mourn
their hands. The worst
isn't that everything might shatter and be lost; the worst
would be to never lose a thing because we've never had it,

just some incomprehensible fear,
far vaster than the universe we know, more catastrophic
than a planet crashing into ours, obliterating it.

Love

You said we would protect each other, we promised
that we wouldn't do each other harm. And it was true. So was the desire
that had you bent over my body like a gardener
clipping at her favorite hedge: the weakest one, of course,
the most susceptible to pests and weather shifts and its own
lacks. You made a vow to me like water and I let
it shelter me, I drank from it, I thought I would—
under your influence and care—be capable of strength,
hostile to any hands beyond your own,
your fingers that would shape our earth,
would give us mulch and food, desolate garden
that we were. And that was when, I'm sure,
a useless passion started growing like
ungovernable ivy: the need to eat each other up,
to slip into the other's body
and never leave, the fight
to sear the fiercest mark onto the other's skin, the one
that would become a stamp of slavery, a master's ownership,
a collar on a beast. That wild,
rabid bolt
demolished all our purest
trust, the kind we knew
as children: that when we woke, the world
would be the same, the house would be exactly where it was
the day before, still orbiting the sun
like every other body in the universe, unknown to us,

not wounding or disturbing us with any
sudden change. Instead, we found
ourselves as errant and unstable as a pair of ghost ships
in the open sea: there'd be no rescue flares
for us, no dazzling sparklers in the sky.
Dry land is far away,
unreachable as constellations
to those of us who wander in a limbo
where our bodies need another body
to feel real. It had been waiting from the start,
the scorpion's tail, taut and arching in the air,
tenacious in its guileless
urge to hurt. The stinger of someone
who loves you knows exactly where
to strike: right in the artery
that pumps the poison through the veins,
replacing in a single violent pulse
your lifeblood's oxygen with the harsh liquid
that will leave you paralyzed. Anyone who has read you
will know your body takes its wounds like words
whose merest mention hurts so fiercely that they're better off unsaid.
And that's the person who can also utter them in such a way
that they won't ever sink back into silence. We said
we'd give each other calm and safety. Instead we both received
a gift no one can ever choose or spurn: the electric shock between the legs,
lethal and unavoidable, when someone comes—
at any cost—to wake you up.

From the Land of the Moon

If, when you met me, you swept me off as the tide sweeps off
a tiny fish, so tired it's nearly dead, should
I say I didn't choose
to follow you? I should. But maybe we forget
the body also has a will
and sometimes that can mean it simply fades
and dies, unless some stronger force,
some energy it can't confront, assails it. You were
that onslaught. Or, in other words, you were the way
life enters dying matter just to shake it up. The scrape
of rock on rock, the mark that one
impenetrable body scrapes onto another
in a brutal crash; the shard, unnoticeably slight, that breaks away,
and which, by breaking, makes the stone
into an object capable of feeling moved by impact, a wounded object
from then on. Isn't illness always just
an unhealed wound, a blemish left so long ago
that we've forgotten it? And isn't love always
the same? Because there is no cure
for what's no longer there: it left, it's floating in
the limbo of the things we fail to see. And this is why
I'm giving you
my illness, this nettled love of life.
Not so you'll heal it, but so you'll do
whatever else you want with it, even make it worse: so love
will turn to rage and to rebellion, and in the end

your mouth will be the thing that downs me whole, the maelstrom
that rises from the ocean floor
and knows no law than the compulsion to devour
the lives it inescapably attracts.

Damage

Sometimes we're rough and cruel as prehistoric beasts,
ungainly, as if we still possessed
the same flawed bodies that have struggled to evolve
with the rest of the species. That still have claws
and fangs and horns. That don't respond to touch
except with blows and scratches. So poor old anyone who comes
anywhere close; poor startled animal that doesn't know
what's coming. Grant me the truce
agreed on by the ones who know the fear
of living, ever threatened
by extinction and obscurity. Just let me rest
here, in the forest, like a deer,
reposing deeply in the way that soothes
its constant vigilance. And if you plan to strike,
then let it be once I'm awake,
in daylight; I don't want death to be
a dream inside another dream. I've felt your body hum
with hate, a baby creature at my chest.
I give myself to you so you can do with me
what you were foiled from doing with your mother
when you were born: I'll be the body you can slash
in order to break free. The one you hurt.
But then I'll stay behind, and lose my way,
because brutality's the form of love
the wounded know, and I won't want

to cause your insides the same pain
that burns in mine. Who could avoid it?
And who could be so good, so selfless, that
they don't return the wrong that was once done to them?
Let's run, me for my life and you for yours, each
to a different far-flung corner of the earth,
never to see each other again. I want
my rage to be the teeth that wrench
the thorn sunk deep into your throat
that stops your breath and prompts this need
to do away with any form
of life. Maybe the one who gives up hatred also gives
up victimhood forever. Victims
don't heal or fix; they're there to be subjected,
sacrificed; they have no other fate. But could
that destiny be different if I forced you to endure
the thing you always fled from: the embrace consumed by pain
and yet still shelters, says: *I loved you,*
I don't care what you've done, I don't care what you do
to me? Maybe it wouldn't. Maybe it just
isn't possible. But all attempts to change the course of what
orbits itself, fixed on an axis that repeats
and always will repeat horrors
and wrongs, are valuable. I'm going
with you, then, as far as I can go,
and I'll leave only when my longing finally becomes the home
you never had, and when your family
has ceased to be the knife-blade at your neck,
tormenting you with every passing day, and has become instead
the red-hot brand, the mark imprinted on the skin
when someone has been rabidly,

intensely loved, and can stop running,
fear and all, because they've found their native land, the country
that was always theirs, although they never knew it until now.

The Edge of Heaven

For she who bows her head is lost and she who meekly lets
herself be caught, steps almost voluntarily
into the slaughterhouse, is dead already. Which
is why I clutched the red-hot iron of your life.
To keep myself from yielding to the jolt of fear, its belly-gash
of spurs. We
don't have a choice. They have no choice,
the mares who canter through the open fields, hell-bent
on just one thing: fleeing their master.
There is a master only if there's prey, if there's a slave,
if there's no flight or battered door collapsed by the incalculable force
of someone's body in revolt. *Don't love me*
like a person, you said to me. Just like that, shyly,
frightened of love as ever, of its caustic substance
scraping anything it touches. *Love*
me like an animal, you said. Let the only thing that matters be
the outbreak driving us from home, out of the species,
the leap that takes us to the other side, the instant when the body hangs
unmoving in midair, utterly free
just as it starts to age,
resign itself.

Only Lovers Left Alive

Teeth marks on your neck: that was love.
Sapped of the blood that let you live,
flooded with emptiness instead, numb liquid
unnourishing. Dying of thirst or hunger unless
you did unto another what was done to you. Feeding on
a body, stripping it with ruthlessness and patience
of the gentle current that carries it away, the placid river
it flows along. But could the ill be cured, the sickness stamped
into you by old teeth, if another body crept into
your own, the particles of both
entwined in such a way
that one life was
inseparable from the other? Could you, I ask, become
the snake that sinks its fangs into my jugular and also bear
the antidote? Would killing
be the same as curing, then; part of
a loop that stops and starts again in the same place,
its own beginning? What if death could be vanquished
by its own weapons flipped, inverted, as if
a crowd of slaves one day resolved to rally
as an army, turning their labor and their strength
against their master? I wanted you to see my blood.
Nothing's more real than that: I could describe
the wound to you, the wound that's in the fibers arching up
like stalks, and breaking sweetly in the iron
that your mouth receives. That is the tang, the texture of my life,

of what was once contaminated. If you could taste it,
would you accept at last that there's no metaphor for this,
and would you understand the sickness comes from love that never sates
the hunger we are born of, and that the cure
is just a keen incision on the site, the cut that frees
the blood contained, the very same
that had amassed inside the heart
and kept it still? Could
you reinvigorate my blood and set the geyser off
to flood me; is such a passion even possible, and can it be
so sure? *Taste me.* Inside the body is the aura
we've been seeking in the spirit, overturning stones,
and it can come back from the dead if it's desired
ferociously enough; it melts
into the fire that burns it off
and never turns to ash.

Nazareno Cruz and the Wolf

Once, seated around a fire, we told each other
the stories we loved. The ones we've repeated
so many times we've come
to believe them. They're neither true nor false, and in the end
it wouldn't matter: who isn't made
of fairy tales. Without them, our bodies would blur
into erasure, light and flimsy
as ash disintegrating in the air. Unlike trees
or animals, we humans have to gather
to be real. When we're together, we look
like more than shadows, we look true, we look like we could last
much longer than the fleeting lapse we really do. How
can such fragile, needy beings cause
such harm? I've often been
the wolf who plucks its prey's heart out and carries it away,
clenched in its jaws; I've roused intolerable pain
where there was only calm,
and not even the flayed animal's howl could halt
the hunting rage in me, the sprinting,
reveled blood, kindled by someone
else's hurt. And what became
of what I loved? My teeth
entrapped it, too. Because
how can a lover ever keep brutality at bay,
eluding violence,

if violence is a bolt that roams the world
and searches for a target, for the magnet that will lure it close,
oblivious to the fire
and hardship it's inviting in? If only the wolf
of us could ever be sated, if thirst
had an end, or a beginning, if we could join
the pack, recover from the craze, the boundless
appetite, the torment of our claws and fangs,
if there were any hope, any at all, that we could stop
damaging others and ourselves, I'd drop it at your feet,
so that you could do with it—my hope—
whatever you wanted: take it into your hands,
toss it aside, let it grow tall
or wilt away. The curse of someone who can't love
is loneliness, and someone who's alone can only act
like wolves: attacking and destroying what she can,
fearing destruction and attacks. And who
can love, who's not alone, if we've been raised
as predators, if all we know is how to claim
our territory? There has to be a way. We have to tell
a story that can save us. The promise,
when disaster strikes, that someone
will always come to rescue us, won't let
us lap the venom from the wound, the poisoned blood that spoils
with hate and spurs revenge. There has to be
a cure. So we won't gash each other's flesh
out of clumsiness or negligence each time we try to touch
again, hoping to give each other
something different than what we've received, something
that can't destroy or be destroyed.
Wouldn't it be beautiful

if we could let go
of these mangled bodies
that see others and the world as rivals
in an arduous, interminable trial—to have
a chest that breathes, a mouth that swallows. In other words,
to survive for no one, for nothing.

Cherry Blossoms

In the blue night
frost haze, the sky glows
with the moon
pine tree tops
bend snow-blue, fade
into sky, frost, starlight.
The creak of boots.
Rabbit tracks, deer tracks,
what do we know.

—Gary Snyder

I wake and think: it's like a tree could
wake in the middle of the night. What do we know?
Locked in our bodies, isolated
from the wondrous things that happen,
unfit to see or feel or even really trust
that they exist at all. What do we know? Maybe the plants rest
too, maybe they have their days or nights of wakefulness, a certain kind
of grief or anguish we will never fully understand,
some touch—the sun, the rain, the wind?—that soothes them.
But let's imagine what an ache must mean to substance
that can't move. Material condemned
to stay right where it is, that has
no way to run or hide. What if the lightning bolt,
the axe, the avalanche, the flood, were not

the only risks to plague it? Let's look
out at the cherry tree, lovely and unparticipating in
the final night of winter. Beyond
the parasitic plants and pests that stifle it, what if
there were some powerful desire that crept along the root
and climbed the battered trunk,
emerging from the leaves and branches, howling
into a silence still impossible to break? What if there were
something that wanted out, that longed to burst into the world,
but doesn't move, stays still and quiet, trapped inside?
Haven't you ever felt like that, immobilized, frozen in place,
totally shattered by another body crushing yours
before it disappears?
I bear the scars,
the marks of your existence. They will fade.
Your voice, your way of uttering even the simplest word
as if it were a song that leaves a wake of beauty once
it's done, a trail unreachable, is nowhere now; it lasted just
as long as what you said. I'm going to live my life
inside the air you spoke into, marked with that wake.
I'm going to live my life just like the tree
that offers you its blossoms once a year, the sole
display of its devotion and its anguish at the world
beyond, at what it lost and can't
recover. Whatever beauty I can manage,
however small and poor, however little it resembles
the white and perfect flowering of the cherry tree, will be for you.
I'll always be what I am now: a branch that works
to bring a bud to blossom, even if it's only one,
to give you one last glimpse
before the winter comes, before
it's drained of sap and strength. That

will be my life: the ardor of
such effort. I know you'll never see
what I can offer you. But here
I'll stay, until I yield, becoming you at last,
until my body brings you back, until my body is
exactly like your own: the mud, the parted trunk, the stripped
dry branch, the petals spent and scattered.

Her

The blessings and the curses dealt in childhood
weren't only physical. It wasn't just the feral marks
of heat or cold for which there is
no suitable relief, or of the unexpected blow, or of a hand's soft touch
that halts the fear. There were words, too,
cascading down like meteorites onto a lone
and helpless planet, a wild flood dispersing craters
on its path through virgin land. You spoke to me
and that lost world returned
as dreams do
when we wake: fragmented, blurry,
and yet all true, as real as any day
we live. I heard your voice, detached
from matter, a resonance
that loses all connection to the mouth that loosed
the sounds it formed.
You spoke to me, I heard
the detonation of a blast that happened far away and long ago,
leaving no trace except the tremors
in my bones. Survivors call out to each other.
At night, when everything they knew
has been wiped out, they fashion cautious codes,
a set of sounds only perceptible to someone else who too
is lost and frightened. I'd recognize
your voice among the rest, its lilt, its slender

hesitation, the faltering before the choice
of certain words, as if language itself had lingered hurt
in you, when you were hurt, and every phrase
a struggle—failed, if beautiful—to seal
the cracks, to wrap what's broken in a wisp of light that keeps it safe
and keeps you safe. Sometimes I can forget
I even have a body when you talk to me:
the particles of me jumble together with your words
and then I'm nothing but the longing for
the ones you give me, like someone with a humble
offering before a sumptuous shrine,
a gift unfitting, and yet a gift that gets it right: it manages to touch
the distant body it adores. *I've never felt a love*
like this before, where are you, please let me in, it's raining
here. I don't want silence. Love's
the faintest conversation, forever on the verge
of dying out, a dialogue heard only by
whoever's in the midst of it, as nothing but
the deep-sea fish can hear the muffled sound
the tides make overhead.
And what would happen if I couldn't hear your voice uprooting me
from shapelessness and giving me a body, what would happen if
there was no life on earth, if beauty and brute force
and the unspeakable intensity of every living thing
had no one to admire them, or quail in fear, or weep with wonder.
Nothing would. If you fell silent, it would open up: the hole
there was before both pain and solace, before
we came into the world, before the oldest versions of the stories that
we've told each other ever since
we understood that telling stories soothes
our fears and draws us close. And even in that emptiness,

what's left of me would listen to your voice as if it were the wind that sweeps away whatever I still had, and that would be just fine. It would be fine for everything to fade out into silence then.

Note

The line "two / despondent children, full of good intentions / but ruled by powers / that we can't fully control" is partly taken from the screenplay of *Persona*, by Ingmar Bergman. The original text reads: "two anxious children, filled with good will and the best intentions, but ruled by powers that we can only partially control."

The poems in this book are based on the following films:

Tomboy, Céline Sciamma, France, 2011

The Silent Touch, Krzysztof Zanussi, UK, 1992

Esteros, Papu Curotto, Argentina, 2016

I Origins, Mike Cahill, US, 2014

Pojkarna, Alexandra-Therese Keining, Sweden, 2015

Hideaways, Angès Merlet, Ireland, 2011

Perfect Sense, David Mackenzie, UK, 2011

Manchester by the Sea, Kenneth Lonergan, US, 2016

4:44 Last Day on Earth, Abel Ferrara, US, 2011

Juste la fin du monde, Xavier Dolan, Canada, 2016

Persona, Ingmar Bergman, Sweden, 1966

Vozvrashchenie, Andrey Zvyagintsev, Russia, 2003

Havnen, Susanne Bier, Denmark, 2010

Gegen Die Wand, Fatih Akin, Germany/Turkey, 2004

Moonlight, Barry Jenkins, US, 2016

Once, John Carney, Ireland, 2007

Pola X, Leos Carax, France, 1999

Magnolia, Paul Thomas Anderson, US, 1999

La belle saison, Catherine Corsini, France, 2015

Melancholia, Lars von Trier, Denmark, 2011

Love, Gaspar Noé, France, 2015

Mal de pierres, Nicole García, France, 2016

Fatale, Louis Malle, France, 1992

Auf der anderen Seite, Fatih Akin, Germany/Turkey, 2007

Only Lovers Left Alive, Jim Jarmusch, UK, 2013

Nazareno Cruz y el lobo, Leonardo Favio, Argentina, 1975

Kirschblüten – Hanami, Doris Dörrie, Germany, 2008

Her, Spike Jonze, US, 2013

About the Author

Claudia Masin, writer and psychoanalyst, was born in Resistencia, Chaco, Argentina, in 1972. She spent 30 years in Buenos Aires before moving to the city of Córdoba, where she currently lives. She coordinates writing workshops and has taught poetry in the writing program at Argentina's National Arts University. Masin is the author of 11 poetry collections, two personal anthologies, and a volume of collected works. Her book *La vista* unanimously won Spain's Casa de América Prize in 2002 and was published by Visor. *Lo intacto* won a prize from the National Arts Fund of Argentina in 2017. Her poem "Tomboy" was among the winners of the 2019 Poems in Translation Prize, organized by Words Without Borders and the Academy of American Poets. Masin's books have been published in Spain, Mexico, Brazil, and Chile; her work is widely anthologized across Latin America and Europe; and her poems have been translated into French, English, Portuguese, Italian, and Swedish.

About the Translator

Robin Myers is a poet, translator, essayist, and 2023 NEA Translation Fellow. Recent translations include *What Comes Back* by Javier Peñalosa M. (Copper Canyon Press); *The Brush* by Eliana Hernández-Pachón (Archipelago Books); *A Whale Is a Country* (Fonograf Editions) and *In Vitro* (Coffee House Press), both by Isabel Zapata; *Copy* by Dolores Dorantes (Wave Books); *The Law of Conservation* by Mariana Spada (Deep Vellum Publishing); and *Bariloche* by Andrés Neuman (Open Letter Books). Her poems have appeared in *Best American Poetry, Yale Review, The Drift, Poetry London,* and elsewhere; her essays, in *Los Angeles Review of Books, Words Without Borders,* and *Latin American Literature Today.*

FLOWERSONG

P R E S S

**FlowerSong Press nurtures essential verse
from, about, and throughout the borderlands.
Literary. Lyrical. Boundless.**

Sign up for announcements about
new and upcoming titles at:

www.flowersongpress.com